Stars

by Grace Hansen

Abdo
OUR GALAXY
Kids

abdopublishing.com

Published by Abdo Kids, a division of ABDO, P.O. Box 398166, Minneapolis, Minnesota 55439.

Copyright © 2018 by Abdo Consulting Group, Inc. International copyrights reserved in all countries. No part of this book may be reproduced in any form without written permission from the publisher.

Printed in the United States of America, North Mankato, Minnesota.

052017

092017

Photo Credits: ESO, iStock, NASA, Shutterstock, ©Ian Norman p.13 / CC-BY-SA 2.0

Production Contributors: Teddy Borth, Jennie Forsberg, Grace Hansen

Design Contributors: Dorothy Toth, Laura Mitchell

Publisher's Cataloging in Publication Data

Names: Hansen, Grace, author.

Title: Stars / by Grace Hansen.

Description: Minneapolis, Minnesota : Abdo Kids, 2018 | Series: Our galaxy |
    Includes bibliographical references and index.

Identifiers: LCCN 2016962403 | ISBN 9781532100512 (lib. bdg.) |
    ISBN 9781532101205 (ebook) | ISBN 9781532101755 (Read-to-me ebook)

Subjects: LCSH: Stars--Juvenile literature.

Classification: DDC 523.8--dc23

LC record available at http://lccn.loc.gov/2016962403

Table of Contents

How Stars Form

Stars are born in cold clouds made of dust and hydrogen. Gravity pulls the cloud together. This causes parts of the cloud to collapse. Small clumps form within the cloud.

5

The clumps begin to spin. The spinning pulls more gas inward. Pressure and heat build within the clumps. **Hydrogen** atoms fuse to form **helium**. A star is born!

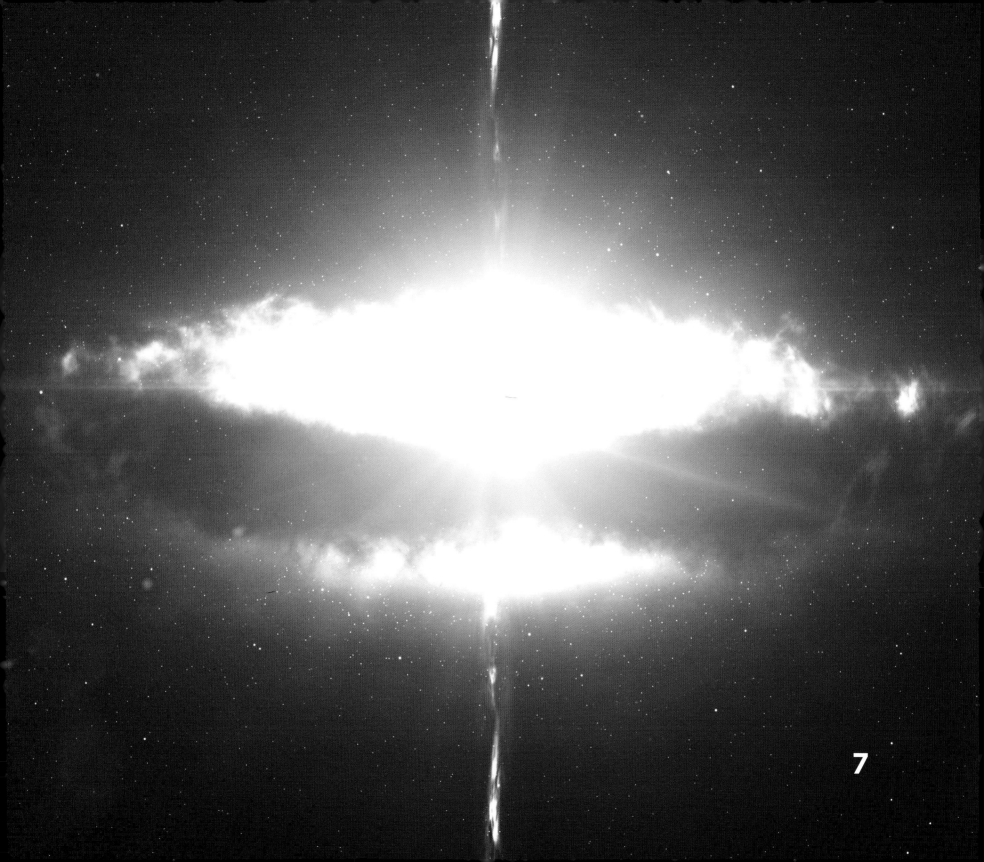

Light and Color

Stars light up the sky. A star makes light in its core. The core makes light by constantly fusing hydrogen into helium.

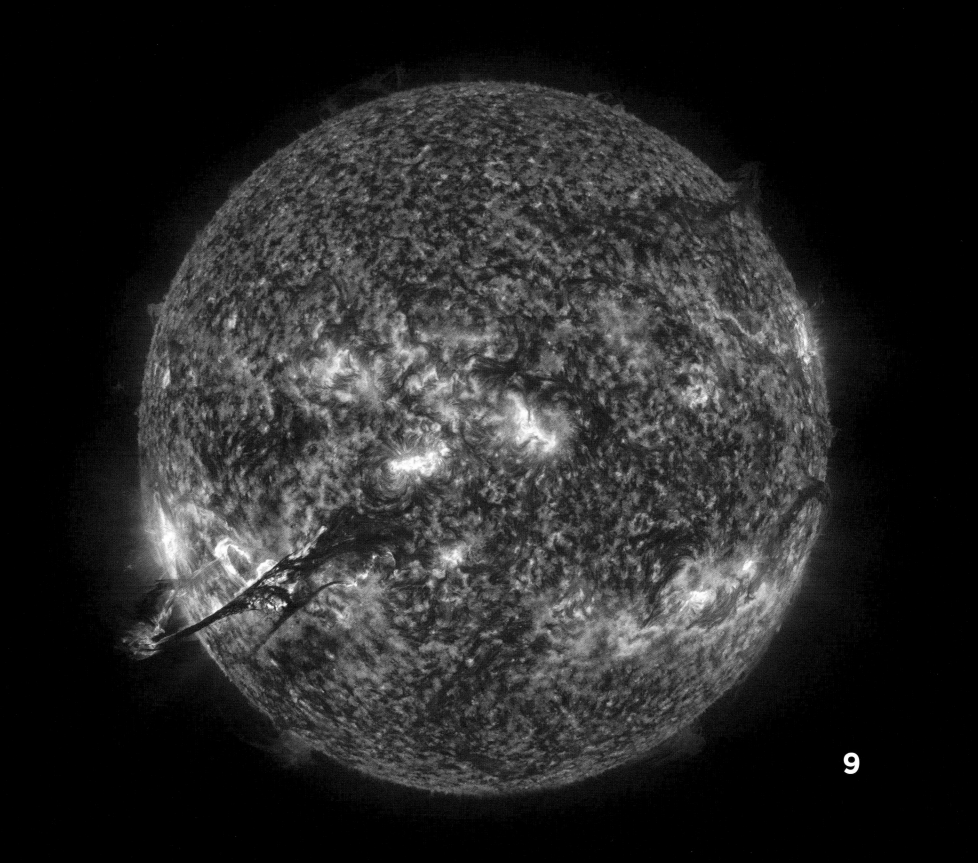

9

Larger stars are brighter and hotter. A huge star puts more pressure on its core. Therefore fusion happens faster. This creates more energy.

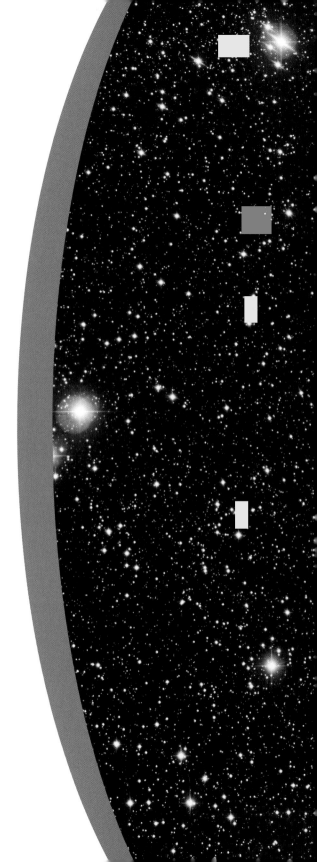

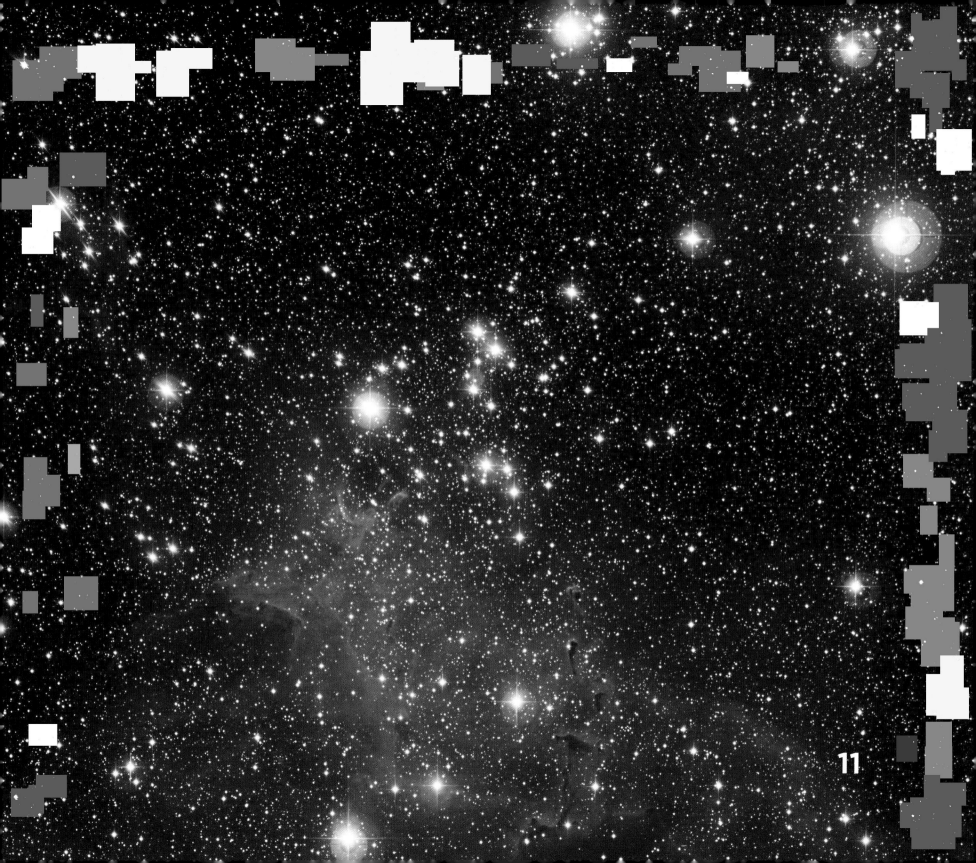

The brightest star in the night sky is Sirius A. It is two times larger than the sun. It is also nearly two times hotter.

Sirius A

Stars come in different colors.
A star's color depends on its
temperature. Hotter stars are
blue or white. Cooler stars
appear yellow, orange, or red.

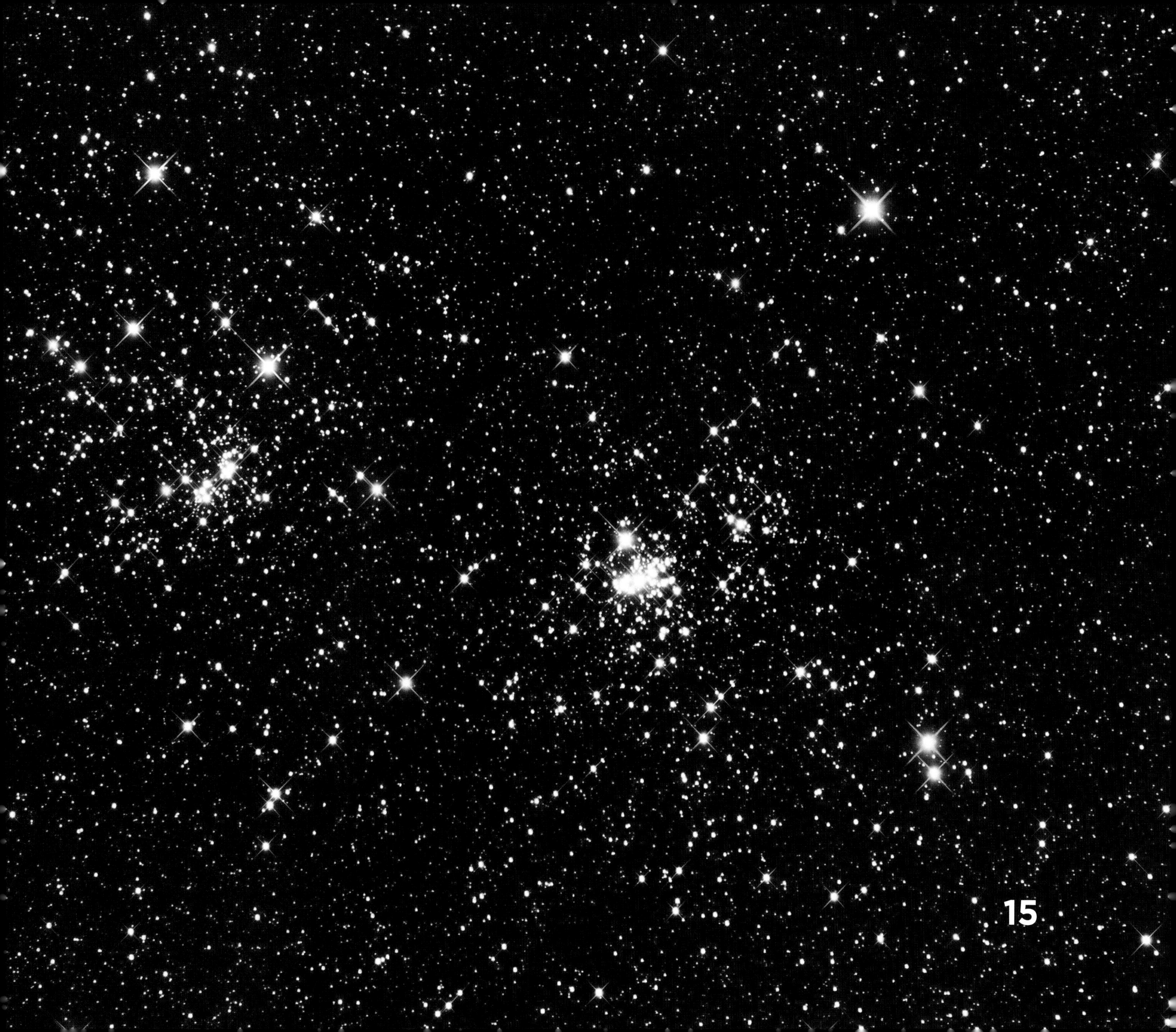

How Stars Die

Stars live for billions of years. At some point, a star's **core** will run out of **hydrogen**. **Gravity** forces the star's core to **collapse**.

Pressure and heat build up. The **core** begins to fuse **helium** into carbon and oxygen. The outer layers of the star **expand**. It becomes a red giant.

red giant

the sun
(current size)

19

Gravity can no longer hold the star together. The star's outer layers drift away. All that is left of the star is its **core**. It is now a white dwarf star. Over millions of years, it will cool down to become a **black dwarf**.

21

More Facts

- There are around 200 to 400 billion stars in the Milky Way.

- Stars look close together when we look up at them. But there are actually huge distances between them. Scientists have compared one star's distance from another star to putting two grains of sand 30 miles (48.3 km) apart.

- Stars live for around 10 billion years.

Glossary

black dwarf – what is left after a white dwarf burns off all of its heat, but retains its mass.

collapse – cave in.

core – a star's center where temperature and pressure are high enough to ignite nuclear fusion, converting atoms of hydrogen into helium.

expand - to become larger or wider.

fusion – a reaction in which the nuclei of light atoms join to form a heavier nucleus, which create a huge amount of energy.

gravity – the force by which all objects in the universe are attracted to each other.

helium – a light, colorless gas that does not burn.

hydrogen – a gas that is lighter than air that catches fire easily.

Index

abdokids.com

Use this code to log on to abdokids.com and access crafts, games, videos and more!

Abdo Kids Code:
OSK0512